UKULELE

Church Songs for KIDS

ISBN 978-1-4803-8286-2

HAL•LEONARD® CORPORATION

7777 W. BLUEMOUND RD. P.O. BOX 13819 MILWAUKEE, WI 53213

In Australia Contact:
Hal Leonard Australia Pty. Ltd.
4 Lentara Court
Cheltenham, Victoria, 3192 Australia
Email: ausadmin@halleonard.com.au

Visit Hal Leonard Online at
www.halleonard.com

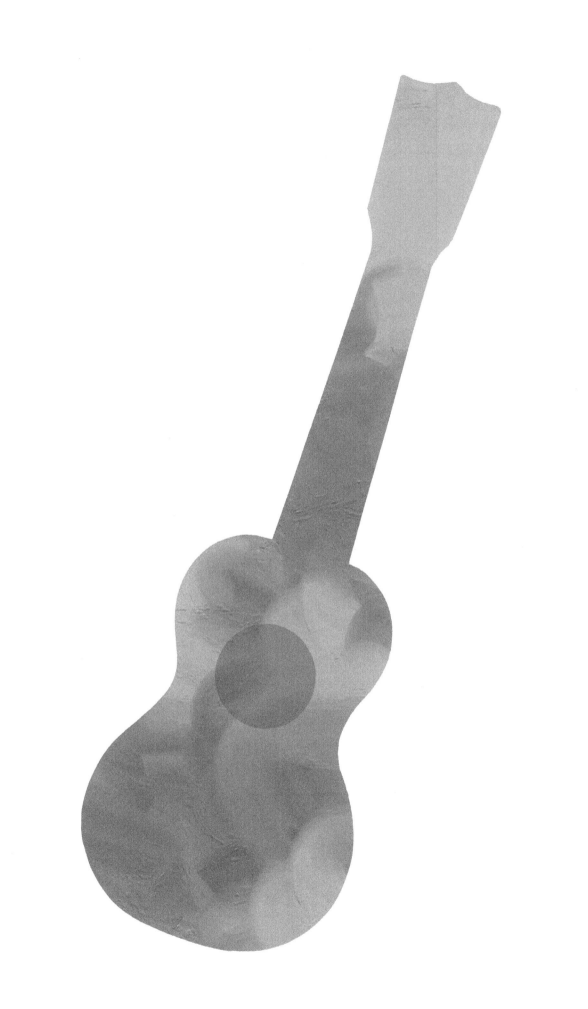

All Night, All Day

Traditional Spiritual

The B-I-B-L-E

Traditional

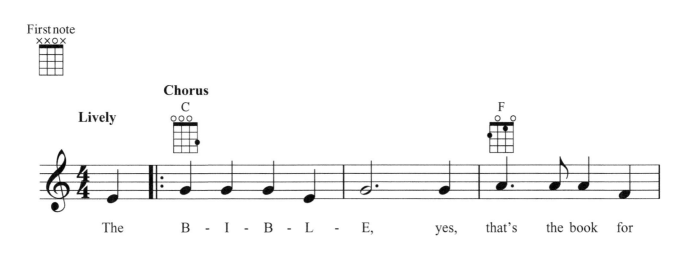

The B - I - B - L - E, yes, that's the book for

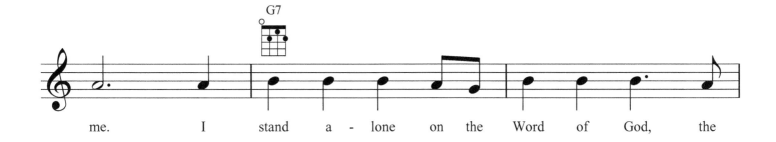

me. I stand a - lone on the Word of God, the

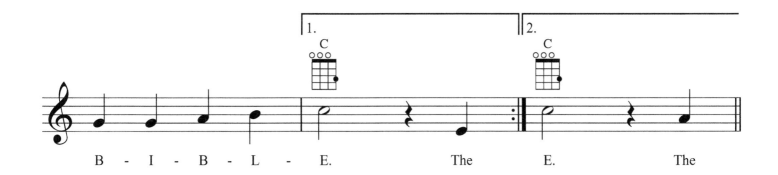

B - I - B - L - E. The E. The

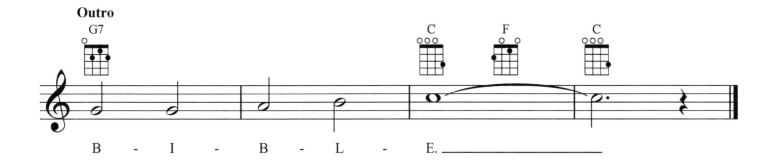

B - I - B - L - E. _____

Arky, Arky

Traditional

First note

Brightly

Verse

1. The Lord __ told No - ah, "There's gon - na be __ a flood - y, flood - y."
(2.–5.) *See additional lyrics*

Lord __ told No - ah, "There's gon - na be __ a flood - y, flood - y.

Get those an - i - mals out of the mud - dy, mud - dy." Chil - dren of the

Chorus

Lord. So rise __ and shine, __ and give God the glo - ry, glo - ry.

Additional Lyrics

2. The Lord told Noah to build him an arky, arky,
   Lord told Noah to build him an arky, arky,
   Build it out of gopher barky, barky,
   Children of the Lord.

3. The animals, the animals, they came in by twosies, twosies,
   Animals, the animals, they came in by twosies, twosies,
   Elephants and kangaroosies, roosies,
   Children of the Lord.

4. It rained and poured for forty daysies, daysies,
   Rained and poured for forty daysies, daysies,
   Almost drove those animals crazies, crazies,
   Children of the Lord.

5. The sun came out and dried up the landy, landy,
   (Look, there's the sun!) It dried up the landy, landy,
   Everything was fine and dandy, dandy,
   Children of the Lord.

Deep and Wide

Traditional

Down in My Heart

Traditional

Do Lord

Traditional

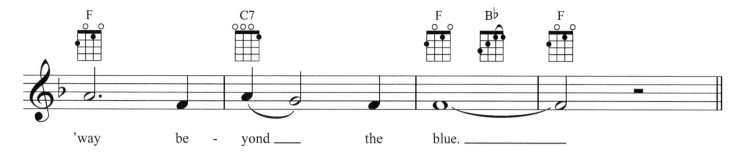

'way   be - yond _____ the   blue. _____

Chorus

Do   Lord,   oh,   do   Lord,   oh,   do   re - mem - ber

me.   Do   Lord,   oh,   do   Lord,   oh,   do   re - mem - ber

me.   Do   Lord,   oh,   do   Lord,   oh,   do   re - mem - ber

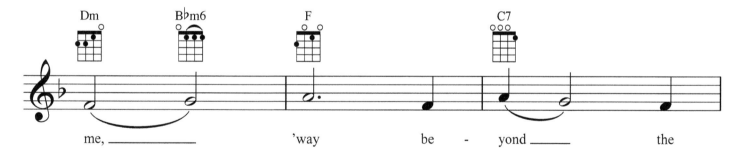

me, _____   'way   be - yond _____ the

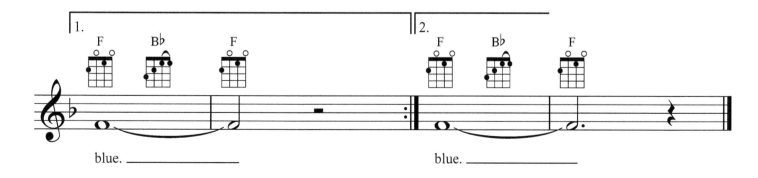

blue. _____   blue. _____

Father Abraham

Traditional

* *Start a continuous motion with the right arm. Add a motion each time a new part of the body is mentioned.*

God Is So Good

Traditional

First note

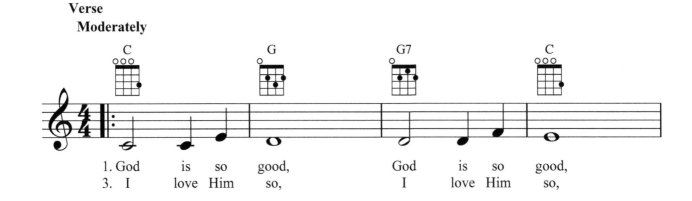

Verse
Moderately

1. God   is   so   good,   God   is   so   good,
3. I   love   Him   so,   I   love   Him   so,

God   is   so   good,   He's   so   good   to   me.
I   love   Him   so,   He's   so   good   to   me.

Verse

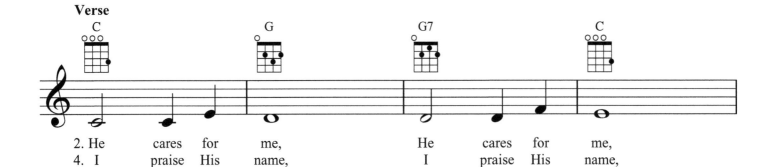

2. He   cares   for   me,   He   cares   for   me,
4. I   praise   His   name,   I   praise   His   name,

1.   2.

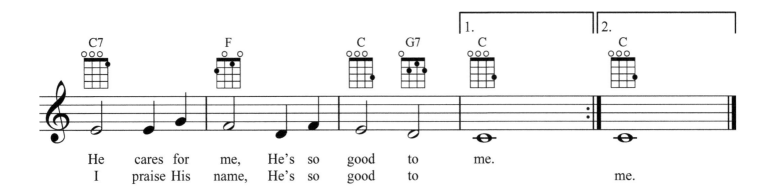

He   cares   for   me,   He's   so   good   to   me.
I   praise   His   name,   He's   so   good   to   me.

Hallelu, Hallelujah!

Traditional

He's Got the Whole World in His Hands

Traditional Spiritual

in His hands. __ He's got the wind and the rain __

in His hands. __ He's got the whole world in His

Verse

hands. 3. He's got ev - 'ry - bod - y here _ in His hands. _ He's got

ev - 'ry - bod - y here _ in His hands. _ He's got ev - 'ry - bod - y here _

in His hands. _ He's got the whole world in His hands.

Ho-Ho-Ho-Hosanna

Traditional

I Am a C-H-R-I-S-T-I-A-N

Traditional

First note

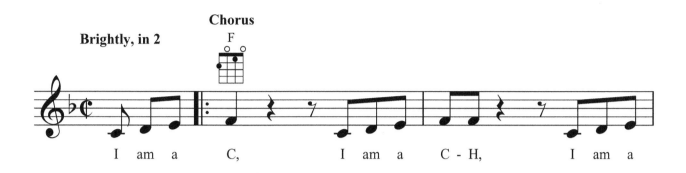

Brightly, in 2   **Chorus**

I am a C,   I am a C - H,   I am a

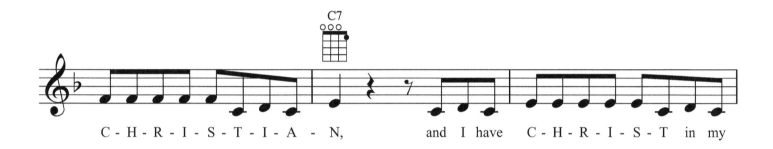

C - H - R - I - S - T - I - A - N,   and I have C - H - R - I - S - T in my

H - E - A - R - T and I will   L - I - V - E   E - T - E - R -

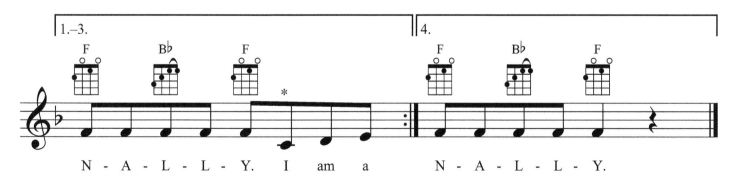

N - A - L - L - Y. I am a   N - A - L - L - Y.

* Speed up on each repeat.

I've Got Peace Like a River

Traditional

If You're Happy and You Know It

Words and Music by L. Smith

Jesus in the Morning

Traditional

First note

Verse
Moderately (♫ = ♩♪)

1. Je - sus, Je - sus,
2. Love ____ Him, love ____ Him,

Je - sus in the morn - ing, Je - sus at the noon - time.
love Him in the morn - ing, love Him at the noon - time.

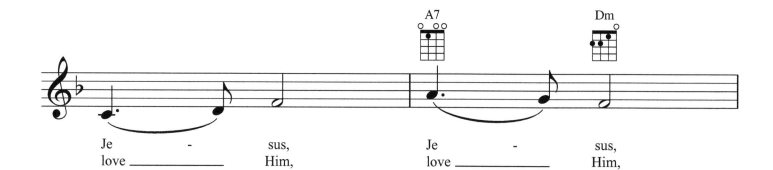

Je - sus, Je - sus,
love ____ Him, love ____ Him,

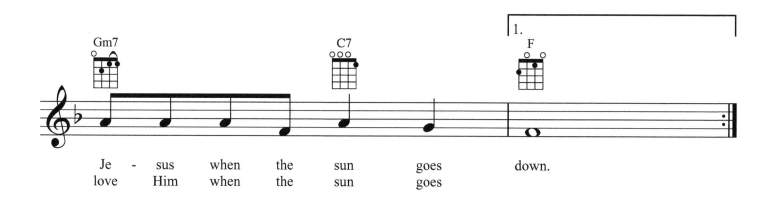

Je - sus when the sun goes down.
love Him when the sun goes

down.

3. Serve _____ Him, serve _____ Him,
4. Praise _____ Him, praise _____ Him,

serve Him in the morn - ing, serve Him at the noon - time.
praise Him in the morn - ing, serve Him at the noon - time.

Serve _____ Him, serve _____ Him,
Praise _____ Him, praise _____ Him,

serve Him when the sun goes down.

praise Him when the sun goes down.

Jesus Loves Me

Words by Anna B. Warner
Music by William B. Bradbury

First note

Verse
Moderately

1. Je - sus loves me; this I know, for the Bi - ble tells me so.
2.–4. *See additional lyrics*

Lit - tle ones to Him be - long; they are weak, but He is strong.

Chorus

Yes, Je - sus loves me! Yes, Je - sus loves me!

Yes, Je - sus loves me; the Bi - ble tells me so.

Additional Lyrics

2. Jesus loves me; He who died,
   Heaven's gates to open wide.
   He will wash away my sin,
   Let His little child come in.

3. Jesus loves me; loves me still,
   Though I'm very weak and ill.
   From His shining throne on high,
   Comes to watch me where I lie.

4. Jesus loves me; He will stay
   Close beside me all the way.
   If I love Him, when I die,
   He will take me home on high.

Jesus Loves the Little Children

Words by Rev. C.H. Woolston
Music by George F. Root

Lord, I Want to Be a Christian

Traditional Spiritual

My God Is So Great, So Strong and So Mighty

Traditional

First note

Chorus
Confidently

My God is so great, so strong and so might-y! There's noth-ing my God can-not

do! My God is so great, so strong and so might-y! There's

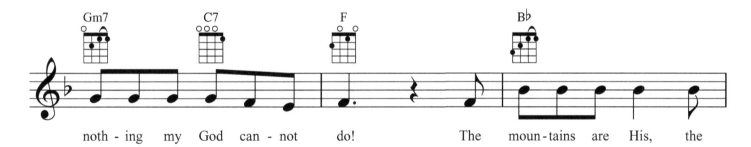

noth-ing my God can-not do! The moun-tains are His, the

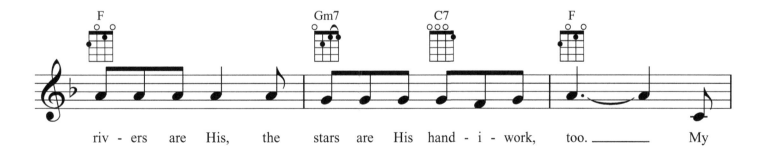

riv-ers are His, the stars are His hand-i-work, too. _____ My

God is so great, so strong and so might-y! There's noth-ing my God can-not do!

Oh, Be Careful

Traditional

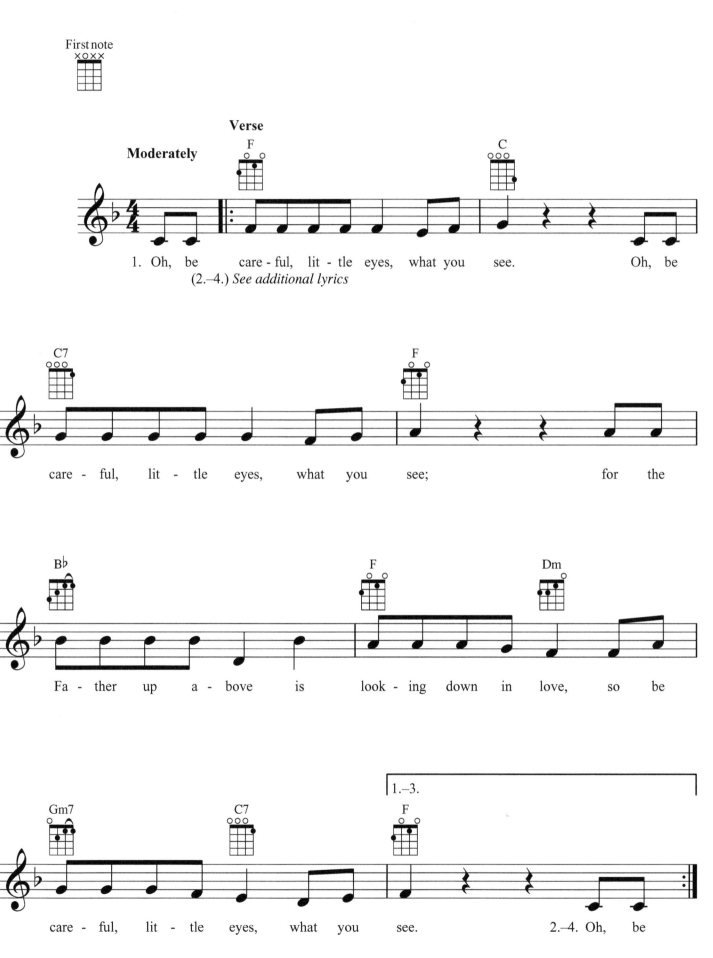

1. Oh, be care-ful, lit-tle eyes, what you see.
(2.–4.) *See additional lyrics*

care-ful, lit-tle eyes, what you see; for the

Fa-ther up a-bove is look-ing down in love, so be

care-ful, lit-tle eyes, what you see. 2.–4. Oh, be

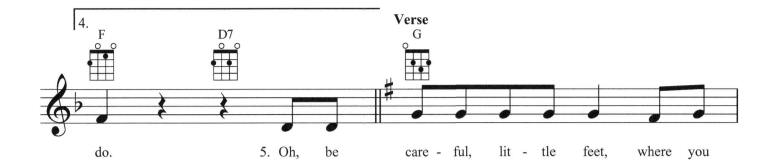

do.   5. Oh, be   care - ful, lit - tle feet, where you

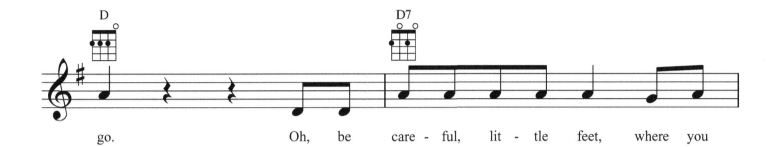

go.   Oh, be   care - ful, lit - tle feet, where you

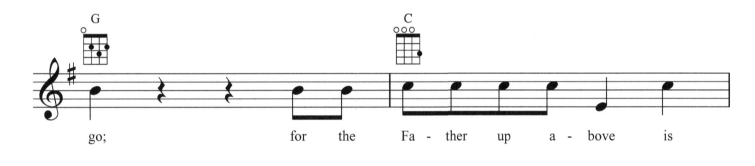

go;   for the Fa - ther up a - bove is

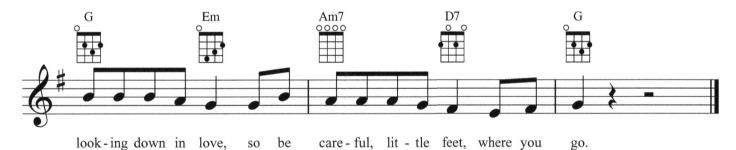

look - ing down in love, so be care - ful, lit - tle feet, where you   go.

Additional Lyrics

2. Oh, be careful, little ears, what you hear.
   Oh, be careful, little ears, what you hear;
   For the Father up above is looking down in love,
   So be careful, little ears, what you hear.

3. Oh, be careful, little tongue, what you say.
   Oh, be careful, little tongue, what you say;
   For the Father up above is looking down in love,
   So be careful, little tongue, what you say.

4. Oh, be careful, little hands, what you do.
   Oh, be careful, little hands, what you do;
   For the Father up above is looking down in love,
   So be careful, little hands, what you do.

Oh, How I Love Jesus

Words by Frederick Whitfield
Traditional American Melody

Praise Him, All Ye Little Children

Traditional Words
Music by Carey Bonner

Rejoice in the Lord Always

Words from Philippians 4:4
Traditional Music

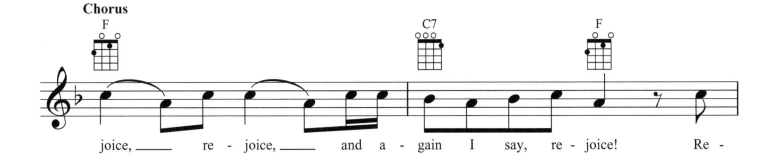

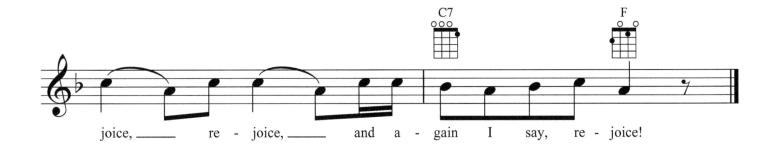

* May be sung as a round.

Thy Word Have I Hid in My Heart

Text based on Psalm 119:11
Music by Earnest O. Sellers

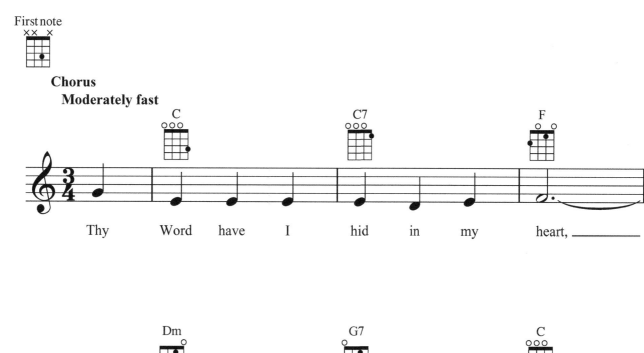

Thy Word have I hid in my heart, _____

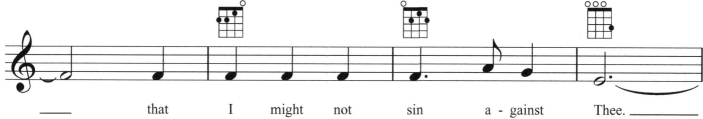

_____ that I might not sin a - gainst Thee. _____

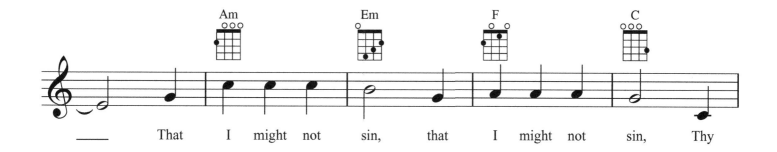

_____ That I might not sin, that I might not sin, Thy

Word have I hid in my heart. _____

This Little Light of Mine

Traditional

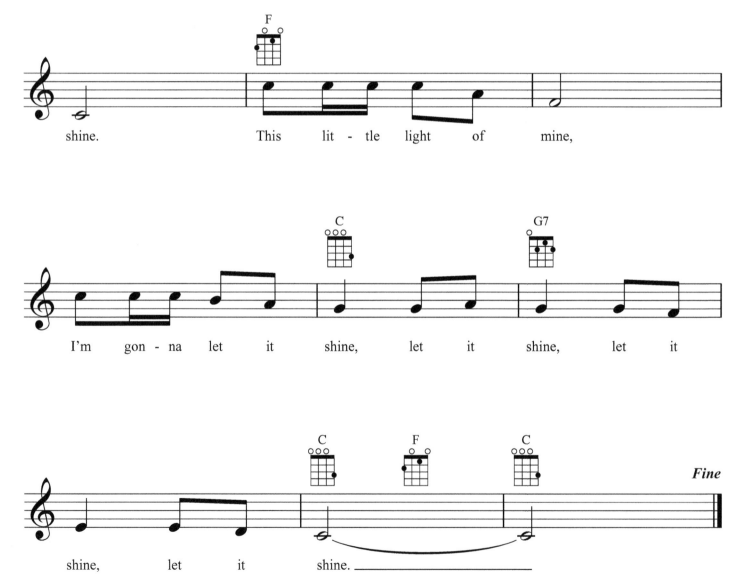

What a Mighty God We Serve

Traditional

Zacchaeus

Traditional

First note
×○××

Verse
Moderately

1. Zac - chae - us was a wee lit - tle man, a wee lit - tle man was
(2.) chae - us knew that he'd done wrong, and sor - ry for his sins was

he. He climbed up in a syc - a-more tree, for the Lord he want - ed to
he. "Lord, to the poor I'll give one half of all my goods," said

see. And as the Sav - ior passed that way, He looked up in the
he. "And if I've cheat - ed an - y - one, four times will I re -

(Spoken:)
tree. *And He said, "Zacchaeus, you come down,* for I'm go - ing to your house to -
pay." *And Jesus said, "Salvation has come to you!* I have come to seek and

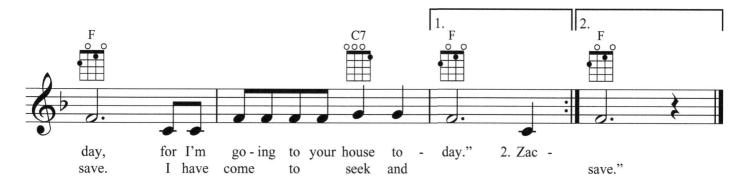

day, for I'm go - ing to your house to - day." 2. Zac -
save. I have come to seek and save."

The Wise Man and the Foolish Man

Traditional

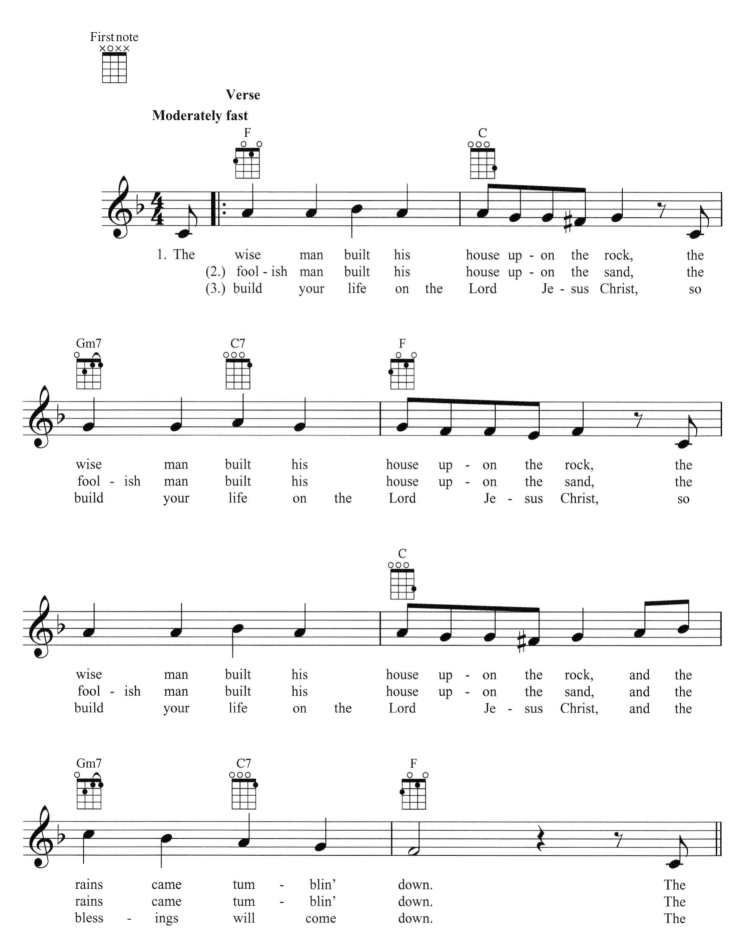

1. The wise man built his house up-on the rock, the
(2.) fool-ish man built his house up-on the sand, the
(3.) build your life on the Lord Je-sus Christ, so

wise man built his house up-on the rock, the
fool-ish man built his house up-on the sand, the
build your life on the Lord Je-sus Christ, so

wise man built his house up-on the rock, and the
fool-ish man built his house up-on the sand, and the
build your life on the Lord Je-sus Christ, and the

rains came tum-blin' down. The
rains came tum-blin' down. The
bless-ings will come down. The

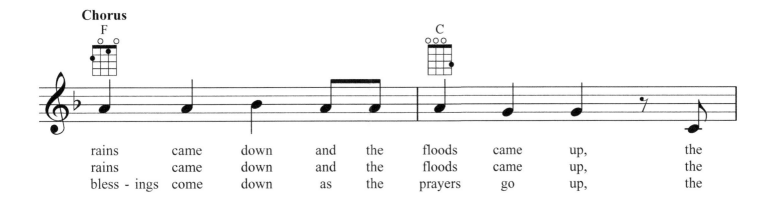

Chorus

rains came down and the floods came up, the
rains came down and the floods came up, the
bless - ings come down as the prayers go up, the

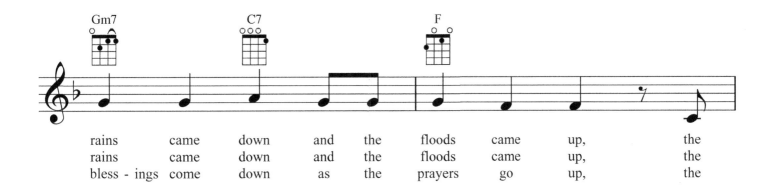

rains came down and the floods came up, the
rains came down and the floods came up, the
bless - ings come down as the prayers go up, the

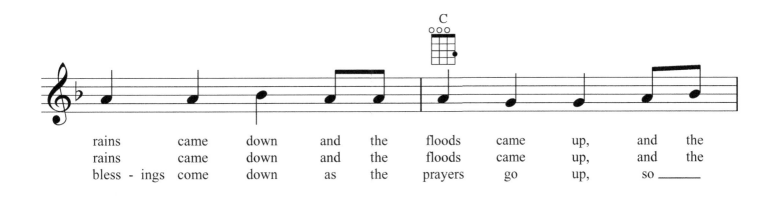

rains came down and the floods came up, and the
rains came down and the floods came up, and the
bless - ings come down as the prayers go up, so ____

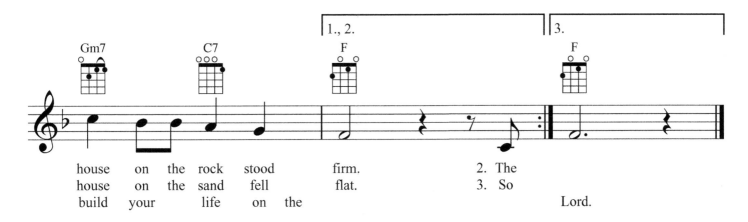

house on the rock stood firm.   2. The
house on the sand fell flat.   3. So
build your life on the   Lord.

Church Music for Kids

CHILDREN'S CHRISTIAN SONGBOOK

Simplified arrangements of 35 favorites: Alive, Alive • Arky, Arky • Deep and Wide • Do Lord • Down in My Heart • Father Abraham • I've Got Peace like a River • I'll Be a Sunbeam • Jesus Loves Me • Jesus Loves the Little Children • Kum Ba Yah • This Little Light of Mine • When the Saints Go Marching In • more!

00702149 Easy Guitar with Notes & Tab..$7.95

THE CHRISTIAN CHILDREN'S SONGBOOK

Easy piano arrangements of 50 songs kids love to sing and play, including: Awesome God • Clap Your Hands • Deep and Wide • Friend of God • Hallelu, Hallelujah! • Here I Am to Worship • I've Got Peace like a River • Jesus Loves the Little Children • More Precious Than Silver • Seek Ye First • Sing to the King • This Is the Day • This Little Light of Mine • Zacchaeus • and more.

00311495 Easy Piano............................$14.95

THE CHRISTIAN CHILDREN'S SONGBOOK

101 songs from Sunday School, all in appropriate keys for children's voices. Includes: Awesome God • The B-I-B-L-E • The Bible Tells Me So • Clap Your Hands • Day by Day • He's Got the Whole World in His Hands • I Am a C-H-R-I-S-T-I-A-N • I'm in the Lord's Army • If You're Happy and You Know It • Jesus Loves Me • Kum Ba Yah • Let There Be Peace on Earth • This Little Light of Mine • When the Saints Go Marching In • more.

00310472 Piano/Vocal/Guitar...............$19.95

EASY HYMNS

arr. Phillip Keveren

20 beloved hymns beautifully arranged by Phillip Keveren, including: All Hail the Power of Jesus' Name • Be Still My Soul • Be Thou My Vision • The Church's One Foundation • Faith of Our Fathers • How Firm a Foundation • I Surrender All • Nearer, My God, to Thee • Softly and Tenderly • 'Tis So Sweet to Trust in Jesus • and more.

00311250 Beginning Piano Solos..........$10.99

EVERLASTING GOD

arr. Phillip Keveren

18 worship songs masterfully arranged for beginning soloists by Phillip Keveren. Includes: Amazing Grace (My Chains Are Gone) • Christ Is Risen • Everlasting God • Forever Reign • Here I Am to Worship • How Great Is Our God • I Will Follow • Indescribable • Mighty to Save • Offering • Sing to the King • Your Grace Is Enough • and more.

00102710 Beginning Piano Solos..........$10.99

MY FIRST HYMN BOOK

12 classic hymns arranged in the user-friendly five-finger format for a great first-time hymn-playing experience! Includes: Amazing Grace • Fairest Lord Jesus • God Is So Good • I Surrender All • I've Got Peace like a River • Jesus Loves Me • Praise Him, All Ye Little Children • Savior, Like a Shepherd Lead Us • Take My Life and Let It Be • and more.

00311873 Five-Finger Piano...................$7.99

MY FIRST WORSHIP BOOK

Beginning pianists will love the five-finger piano format used in this songbook featuring eight worship favorites: Friend of God • Give Thanks • Here I Am to Worship • I Will Call Upon the Lord • More Precious Than Silver • Sing to the King • We Fall Down • You Are My King (Amazing Love).

00311874 Five-Finger Piano...................$7.99

SACRED VOCAL SOLOS FOR KIDS

WITH A CD OF PIANO ACCOMPANIMENTS

30 songs of faith in easy arrangements. Includes: Amazing Grace • He's Got the Whole World in His Hands • Jesus Loves Me • Simple Gifts • and many more.

00110424 Piano/Vocal...........................$22.99

SCRIPTURE SONGS FOR CHILDREN'S CHURCH

by Pendleton Brown
Book/CD Pack

Pendleton Brown has set 40 popular Bible verses to music, creating a fun and effective way to memorize them! This book includes melody, lyrics and chords as well as a sing-along CD. Songs include: Cast Your Cares on the Lord (Psalm 55:22) • Follow the Way of Love (1 Corinthians 14:1) • Man Does Not Live by Bread Alone (Matthew 4:4) • Walk in the Spirit (Galatians 5:16) • and more.

00316689 Melody/Lyrics/Chords.........$14.99

SCRIPTURE SONGS FOR KIDS

Big-note arrangements of 16 great songs, each complete with scripture references. Includes: As the Deer • Create in Me a Clean Heart • He Is Good • Love the Lord • Seek Ye First • This Is the Day • Thy Word • and more. A wonderful resource for Sunday School!

00311994 Big-Note Piano.......................$9.99

WORSHIP HITS FOR UKULELE

25 unique uke arrangements, including: Above All • Cornerstone • Everlasting God • Forever • God Is Able • The Heart of Worship • Hosanna • I Give You My Heart • Jesus Messiah • Our God • Overcome • Revelation Song • The Stand • 10,000 Reasons (Bless the Lord) • Your Grace Is Enough • and more.

00123535 Ukulele $12.99

WORSHIP SONGS FOR UKULELE

25 church favorites arranged for uke, including: Amazing Grace (My Chains Are Gone) • Blessed Be Your Name • Come, Now Is the Time to Worship • Everyday • God of Wonders • Here I Am to Worship • How Great Is Our God • Lord, I Lift Your Name on High • Mighty to Save • Open the Eyes of My Heart • Sing to the King • We Fall Down • You Are My King (Amazing Love) • You're Worthy of My Praise • and more.

00702546 Ukulele $12.99